You Choose

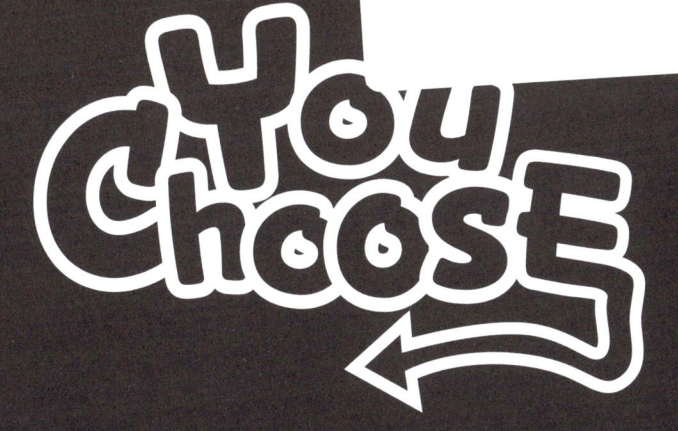

Space

SONYA NEWLAND

WAYLAND

First published in Great Britain in 2024 by Wayland
Copyright © Hodder and Stoughton Limited, 2024

Produced for Wayland by
White-Thomson Publishing Ltd
www.wtpub.co.uk

All rights reserved.

Editor: Sonya Newland
Series Designer: Rocket Design (East Anglia) Ltd

HB ISBN: 978 1 5263 2427 6
PB ISBN: 978 1 5263 2645 4

MIX
Paper from responsible sources
FSC® C104740

Wayland
An imprint of
Hachette Children's Group
Part of Hodder & Stoughton
Carmelite House
50 Victoria Embankment
London EC4Y 0DZ
An Hachette UK Company
www.hachettechildrens.co.uk

Printed in China

Picture acknowledgements:
Shutterstock: ahmadalfant 4, 5, nat sam 4t, Net Vector 5t, Aluna1 6, bsd studio 7, helgascandinavus 8, mhatzapa 9, Barnawi M Thahir 10t, YOK85 10b, kortio 12, Luftside 13, 18l, 19l, Anton Brand 14, tuzudesign 15, Abi pandu wiguna01 16, The Creative Guy 17, Lemonade Serenade 18r, 19r, aksol 20, 21, alex74 22, Pro Symbols 23, galacticus 24, 25, 28, 65, 78, Drekhann 26, shaineast 27, Golden Shrimp 30, tutsi 31, 32, ArtMari 33, Melok 34–35, 60, i n s a n e 36, lineartestpilot 37, 38, 54, 90, Cory Thoman 39, G.roman 41, theerakit 42, Scc.comics 43, Lulus Budi Santoso 44, nawaz sharif 45, Nikolamirejovska 46, Irina Kryvets 47, LUDmyla 48, Daniela Barreto 49, Angelina De Sol 50, Catalyst Labs 51, kristinasavkov 52, Padma Sanjaya 53, Christos Georghiou 56, MarinaTab 57, candesign 59, frozenbunn 61t, 64, MaxNadya 61b, 32 pixels 62, 63, halimqd 66, mijatmijatovic 67, shooarts 68, 69, WinWin artlab 70, Martina V 71, Uncle Leo 72, zizi_mentos 73, Blue bee 74, Natalya Maevskaya 75l, Olha Saiuk 75r, pikepicture 76, Luis Line 77, Maksymkina Yuliia 79, jsabirova 80, tiny_selena 81, Andiz.od 82, tutsi 83, Gwens Graphic Studio 84, 85, Morphart Creation 86, Minh Do 88, klyaksun 89, LHF Graphics 91.

All design elements from Shutterstock.

Every effort has been made to clear copyright. Should there be any inadvertent omission, please apply to the publisher for rectification.

The website addresses (URLs) included in this book were valid at the time of going to press. However, it is possible that contents or addresses may have changed since the publication of this book. No responsibility for any such changes can be accepted by either the author or the publisher.

All facts and statistics were correct at the time of press.

In this book, you get to choose between two options about space (neither of them usually very nice!). Study the pros and cons before making up your mind. Along the way, you'll discover some bizarre, hilarious and disgusting facts about how to survive in space.

Be frozen or fried?
OUCH!

Burp or fart in space?
YUCK!

Spacewalk or moonwalk?
NO WAY!

Live on the Moon or Mars?
HELP!

You choose!

Would you rather go on holiday to Venus ...

Remember to wear a sun hat!

You might think that Mercury is the hottest planet in the Solar System because it's closest to the Sun. But you'd be wrong! Venus holds that title thanks to its incredibly thick atmosphere. Just like here on Earth, greenhouse gases build up in the atmosphere, trapping heat and warming up the planet.

The difference is that on Venus, so much gas gets trapped that it creates a 'runaway greenhouse effect'. The result is surface temperatures of around 475° Celsius – that's hot enough to melt the metal lead!

... or Uranus?

Don't forget your thermal underwear!

Brrrrr!

Uranus and Neptune try to outdo each other to be crowned 'coldest planet', and there's not much in it most of the time. As the furthest planet from the Sun, Neptune might seem the obvious winner, but in fact Uranus, at a mere 2.9 billion kilometres from the Sun, has the lowest temperature ever recorded, −224° Celsius.

Scientists think that Uranus is so chilly because at some point in its past, an asteroid or other space body smashed into it and knocked the heat out of it.

YOU CHOOSE Burn to a crisp or freeze solid?

Would you rather dodge rocks ...

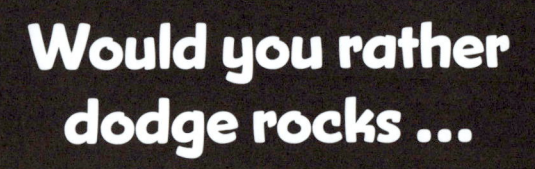

Play 'avoid the asteroid'!

Swirling around in between the orbits of Jupiter and Mars lies the Asteroid Belt. It contains over 1.1 million asteroids over 1 kilometre in diameter, millions of smaller asteroids, and the dwarf planet Ceres. The biggest asteroid is 4 Vesta, which is about 525 kilometres across!

It sounds dangerous, but objects in the Asteroid Belt are spaced really far apart – on average there are about 1 million kilometres between them! If you gathered them all up and squashed them together into a ball, it would be smaller than the Moon.

... or ice blocks?

Stand by for an icy onslaught!

The Kuiper Belt, far out in the Solar System beyond Neptune, is much bigger than the Asteroid Belt. It contains millions of icy space objects and more than a trillion comets. Many of the comets we see come from the Kuiper Belt.

The best-known inhabitant of the Kuiper Belt is Pluto – the planet that famously got demoted from planet to dwarf planet! Some space scientists think that the Kuiper Belt might contain another planet, but 'Planet 9' is yet to be found.

YOU CHOOSE Risk your life in the Asteroid Belt or the Kuiper Belt?

Would you rather see the birth of a star ...

Baby stars all over the place!

Nebulae are huge clouds of gas and dust in space. That doesn't sound like anything special, but amazing things can happen in a nebula. Sometimes all the dust and gases, such as hydrogen and helium, start clumping together. The more mass the clumps get, the more gravity they have.

Eventually, they get so big that they collapse from their own gravity. The matter at the centre of the clump gets very, very hot – and that's the start of a new star. No wonder nebulae are nicknamed 'star nurseries'.

... or the death of one?

Shooting shock waves!

A supernova is the dramatic death of a massive star. It happens when a star runs out of fuel. As it cools, gravity eventually win its fight to squeeze the star's matter into the smallest space possible. The whole thing collapses suddenly, sending out shock waves that create a massive explosion.

Of course, it's hard to see a supernova. You'd have to be looking in exactly the right place at exactly the right time. And in the last thousand years, only five supernovae have occurred that are visible to the naked eye!

You Choose — Visit a star nursery or witness a supernova?

Would you rather experience gravity on the Moon ...

One giant leap ...

Gravity is the force that pulls all objects towards each other. It's what keeps the planets moving around the Sun, the Moon moving around Earth, and your feet on the ground!

Because the Moon is much smaller than Earth, gravity there is only about one-sixth of the strength it is on Earth. That means you could jump six times as high on the Moon as you can on Earth!

Arghhh – I can't take the pressure!

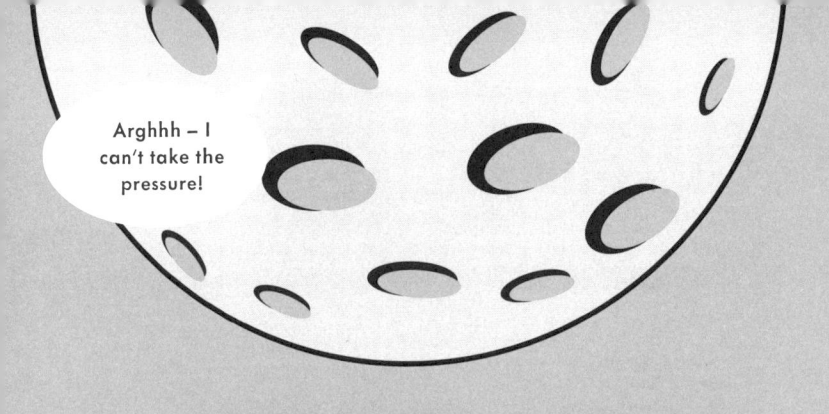

... or on Jupiter?

You'd definitely feel the pressure!

Jupiter is massive! In fact, its mass is more than 2.5 times the mass of all the other planets put together. That gives it greater gravity, too. Jupiter's gravity is so strong that it breaks apart things like comets that get too close, and pulls the pieces into orbit around it.

Gravity on Jupiter is 2.4 times that on Earth. If you paid a visit to Jupiter, the strong pull of gravity between you and the planet would make you feel much heavier.

YOU CHOOSE Do the high jump or feel the weight of a world on your shoulders?

Would you rather encounter a rogue planet ...

Watch out for space wanderers

Rogue planets are similar to the planets in our own Solar System, but they don't orbit a star like ours do. They've somehow floated away from their own solar system and are drifting around in space all on their own.

Well, sort of on their own. Until recently, scientists hadn't identified many rogue planets, but in 2021 they found a whole gang of them – more than 70 in all! All of them have masses similar to Jupiter's.

... or a dwarf planet?

This would be a rare sighting

Dwarf planets are too small to be proper planets, but too big to fit in a group with any other type of space body. A dwarf planet must orbit the Sun and have enough gravity to have formed a ball shape, but must not be big enough to have cleared away nearby objects from its orbit.

I'm a bit special!

You might think that plenty of objects in space would fit those criteria, but it's an exclusive club. There are only five confirmed dwarf planets in the whole Solar System: Pluto, Eris, Haumea, Makemake and Ceres.

YOU CHOOSE Cross paths with a weird planet or a very rare one?

Would you rather burp in space ...

Experience some sick science

You can't really burp in space. On Earth, gravity pulls food and liquid in your stomach further down, but gases stay higher up. That means the air can pop back up your throat and come out as a burp.

In space, you feel weightless as you float around. After eating, this causes any gases to mix together with the food and liquid in mushy chunks in your stomach. If you burped, those chunks would all come up together. Sound familiar? Yep, burping in space is like being sick in your mouth.

Get me out of here!

... or fart in zero gravity?

Surrounded by your own stink!

You can break wind in zero gravity, but it's not a pleasant experience – especially for everyone around you. On Earth, a fart floats off into the air and disappears, but in space the gas (and the smell) just hangs around ...

Farts can also be a fire hazard! Bacteria in the stomach create the gases hydrogen and methane, both of which can catch fire. Which isn't what you want in space.

YOU CHOOSE A nasty taste in your mouth or a nasty smell in the air?

Would you rather wish on a shooting star ...

See a streaker in the sky

A shooting star, sometimes called a falling star, actually isn't a star at all. Those flashes you see in the sky are actually caused by meteoroids. These small bits of dust and rock enter Earth's atmosphere, where they burn up to create a brief trail of light, called a meteor.

Meteoroids are very hot – about 1,650° Celsius. And they travel at about 70 kilometres per second. So, you probably shouldn't catch one and put it in your pocket like the famous song suggests!

... or be there for a blue moon?

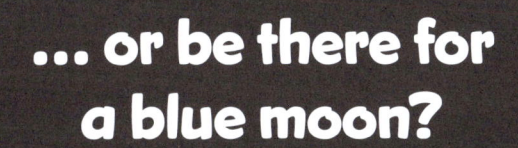

It's nothing to do with the colour

Have you ever heard someone refer to a 'blue moon'? Do you think that on these odd occasions the Moon actually turns blue? If so, you'd be wrong!

Most of the time, there are three full moons in a season. But occasionally, a season will have four full moons, and the fourth one is known as a blue moon. Blue moons only occur every two or three years, so you'll have to wait a while to see one.

YOU CHOOSE Have a wish granted or see something rather rare?

Would you rather stand on Mercury ...

Keep your feet on solid (but scorching) ground

Mercury is the smallest planet. At 15,329 kilometres all the way round, it's only a bit bigger than Earth's Moon. It's a rocky planet with a solid surface, so, practically speaking, there's nothing to stop you standing on it.

However, Mercury has a few features that might put you off taking a stroll, including the fact that it has no atmosphere. That means there's nothing to protect you from the Sun's fierce rays. Also, breathing might be tricky!

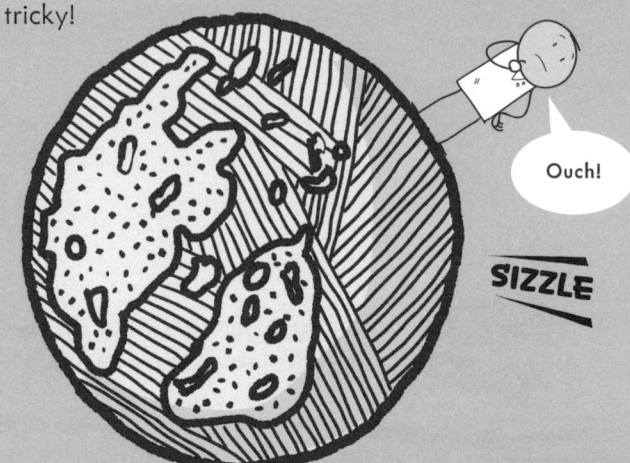

I'm getting that sinking feeling!

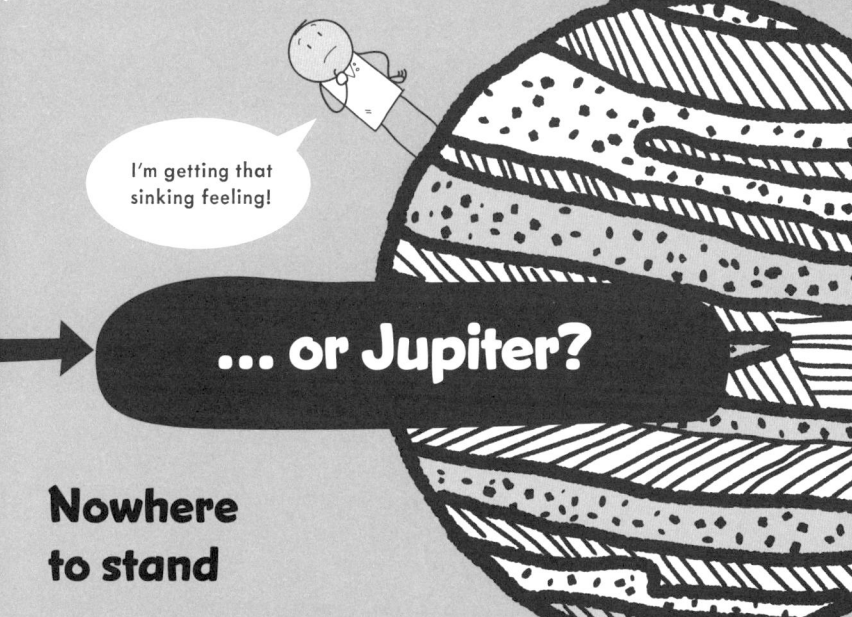

... or Jupiter?

Nowhere to stand

With a circumference of 439,264 kilometres, Jupiter is the largest planet – but that doesn't mean there's plenty of standing room. Jupiter is a 'gas giant', without any solid surface at all.

Jupiter is mostly made up of hydrogen and helium. Deep down, the temperature and pressure increase so much that the hydrogen turns to liquid, creating a huge ocean. That pressure would also crush anything that got too close.

YOU CHOOSE Get zapped by the Sun's rays or sink into a ball of gas?

Would you rather follow a comet ...

Haven't we been here before?

Comets are debris made of ice, rock and dust, left over from when the Solar System formed. Like planets, comets orbit the Sun on a regular, repeating route for centuries. The path of a comet is highly elliptical (very elongated).

When a comet gets closer to the Sun, some of its ice starts to melt and turn to gas, which – along with a trail of dust – creates the long tail you can see when a comet passes by.

... or hitch a ride on a meteoroid?

Incoming!

Heading for disaster

Meteorites are bits of comets, asteroids or meteoroids that fall to Earth. They somehow survive passing through our atmosphere without burning up, and land on the surface of our planet.

Scientists get excited about meteorites because they're so old. By studying what meteorites are made of, we can find out loads about how the Solar System, planets, asteroids and other space bodies formed.

YOU CHOOSE Go round in circles or come in for a crash landing?

21

Would you rather try to find north on Venus ...

Which way is up?!

Venus is a topsy-turvy planet. Scientists think that at some point in its past, another big space body collided with it, knocking it over. It spins clockwise on its axis, not anticlockwise like most of the other planets.

Orienteering on Venus would also be difficult because you couldn't use a compass to find your way. The planet rotates too slowly to create a magnetic field.

... or navigate around Uranus?

See everything sideways

Like Venus, Uranus spins clockwise. But it also has a weird 'tilt'. Rather than being upright, the planet is on its side. It was probably knocked that way by a space collision millions of years ago.

Uranus's unusual position gives it other unique features. For example, while Saturn, Jupiter and Neptune all have horizontal rings, Uranus has vertical ones!

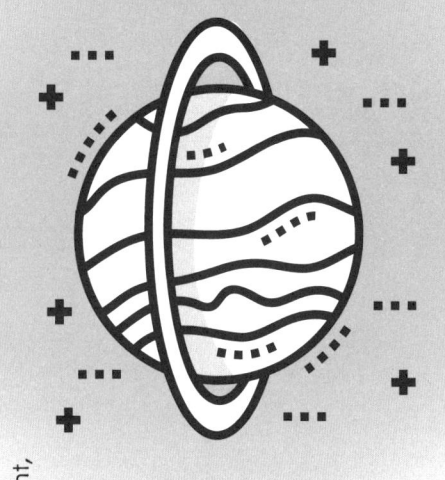

YOU CHOOSE Go north when you want to go south or go east when you want to go west?

Would you rather live on the Moon ...

Know it's a short trip home

If you're thinking of setting up home in another part of the Solar System, the Moon might be a good choice. It's only three days' journey by spaceship to get home for a visit. And you'd still be able to see Earth.

The drawbacks? One day on the Moon is 29.5 Earth days, which might get confusing. You wouldn't have much choice in what to wear on the Moon, as it has a very thin atmosphere, called an exosphere, so a spacesuit is vital for survival. Also, if you like gravity, there's not much to go around on the Moon!

Hi Mum, should be home tomorrow – er, I mean next month!

... or on Mars?

I can almost see home!

Enjoy a more Earth-like environment

Mars is a lot further away. In fact, a trip home to see the family would take about nine months. If you stood on Mars and stared at the sky, you might be able to see Earth, but it would be no more than a dot.

On the upside, one day on Mars is about the same as on Earth, so there wouldn't be so much calendar confusion. It's also rocky, like Earth, so you can stand on it. Gravity on Mars isn't as strong as on Earth, but it's stronger than on the Moon!

YOU CHOOSE Settle close to home or travel further afield for a more Earth-like experience?

Would you rather learn from a distant space probe ...

A one-way trip to the stars

The two unpiloted Voyager space probes were launched in the 1970s. They've been sending information about the planets they passed back to Earth for more than 45 years.

Now more than 22 billion kilometres from Earth, they will soon run out of fuel. But the information they've provided has taught us a lot. The probes have travelled further and seen more of our universe first-hand than any other human-made object.

... or a planetary explorer?

Researching remote rocks

The Mars rovers are a series of robotic vehicles that have been sent to the Red Planet. Their mission is to research conditions there to help scientists learn more, and to see if human astronauts could one day go there themselves.

The rover Perseverance landed on the planet in 2021. Earlier rovers found evidence that there was once water on Mars, so Perseverance is looking for signs of ancient life, as well as collecting rock samples.

YOU CHOOSE Investigate interstellar space or explore a planet we might one day live on?

Would you rather hang out at an event horizon ...

Get drawn into the darkness

An event horizon is an area around a black hole. Beyond this boundary, nothing – not even light – can escape the powerful gravity. Anything that passes across the event horizon has no choice but to move towards the hole.

If you saw something moving towards an event horizon, you'd notice an odd effect. The object would appear to move more and more slowly as it approached, but you would never see it actually reach the horizon. That's because the gravity of the black hole slows down time around it!

... or venture into the twilight zone?

Chase the dawn

If you look at pictures of Earth from space, you might see a fuzzy line of light. On one side, the planet looks dark and on the other, light. That line is known as the terminator, or the twilight zone.

The terminator is the line that separates the daylit and night-time parts of the planet, and it's constantly on the move. It looks fuzzy because Earth's atmosphere bends sunlight.

YOU CHOOSE Take a step into the darkness or never quite catch up with the light?

Would you rather be a low-orbit litter collector ...

No dustbins in space!

Litter is a big problem here on Earth, but did you realise it's also an issue in space? There's loads of human-made junk floating around up there. And all of it can be hazardous, whether it's a big chunk of an old satellite or a small flake of paint.

Most space junk falls to Earth, but that doesn't happen immediately. It might be stuck in orbit for centuries! There have been several incidents where space junk has collided with active satellites.

... or a cleaner on a space station?

It's a messy job ...

It's important to keep things clean on a space station. Just think how messy it would be if astronauts let bits of food, drink and bodily fluids float around! Worse, a type of fungus has been found to thrive in space, especially on the space station.

Astronauts are expected to keep things clean. They wipe down surfaces with special fluid to get rid of microbes and make sure that equipment doesn't get mouldy. Space stations also have air-filtering systems to keep things dust-free.

YOU Choose

Clear up the debris of decades from space litterbugs or chase after floating food and fungus?

Would you rather be stuck in a downpour of liquid metal ...

You'll need more than an umbrella here!

Exoplanets are planets that are outside our own Solar System. WASP-76 b is a huge exoplanet. To give you an idea of how huge, it's about twice the size of Jupiter, which is itself 11 times the size of Earth!

But its size isn't WASP-76 b's only impressive feature. It's so hot there that iron on the planet melts and turns to vapour. Just like in the water cycle on Earth, the vapour rises and moves in the atmosphere. When it reaches a cooler part of the planet, the iron turns back into liquid and falls as deadly metal rain!

... or a shower of liquid glass?

No shelter from the shards

From a distance, exoplanet HD 189733 b looks like a calm blue planet. But don't be fooled – the weather there can be a killer! To begin with, the wind on HD 189733 b whirls at around seven times the speed of sound.

But that's not the worst of it. Scientists think that the chemical composition of the planet could mean that it rains glass! And those high winds would make the rain slash sideways at high speeds.

YOU CHOOSE
Death by a thousand stabs or a thousand cuts?

Would you rather race around Saturn's rings ...

Stay in your lane!

Saturn is well known for its rings, but what exactly are these famous features? Well, they're pieces of comets, asteroids and broken moons that got too close to the planet and were pulled into orbit by its gravity.

All the rings race around at different speeds and are different widths. The main rings are a massive 270,000 kilometres across. The pieces range in size from teeny particles of dust to massive chunks as big as a mountain!

JUPITER

... or take a tour of Jupiter's moons?

An ever-increasing collection

Jupiter has 92 known moons at the last count! Twelve new ones were discovered as recently as 2021–22, so there may be more still to be found.

Not all of Jupiter's moons have officially been named. But of the ones that have, the four most famous are Io, Europa, Ganymede and Callisto. These were first spotted by Italian astronomer Galileo in 1610.

SATURN

YOU CHOOSE Ride round a rocky racetrack or stroll around a moon museum?

35

Would you rather travel at the speed of light ...

Travel light!

Out in space, distances between stars and galaxies are so vast that it doesn't make sense to measure them in kilometres. Instead, scientists use light years. Light travels at 300,000 kilometres per second, and one light year is about 9.46 trillion kilometres. You could get to Proxima Centauri, our nearest neighbouring star, in 4.3 light years!

Unfortunately, we'll never know what it's like to travel that fast, because it would take an infinite amount of energy. But at nearly the speed of light, time would slow down and you would see everything as if through a tunnel-shaped window.

... or travel through a wormhole?

Take a shortcut

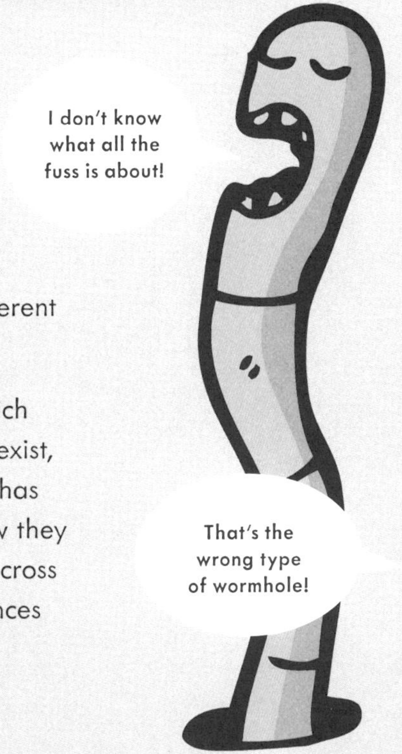

You can imagine a wormhole as a tunnel that connects two points in space. Some scientists believe that wormholes start at a black hole and end at a white hole in a different point in space-time.

I don't know what all the fuss is about!

Wormholes are hypothetical, which means that although they might exist, no one has ever found one. Nor has anyone been able to explain how they might form. But if you do come across one, you could travel huge distances really quickly!

That's the wrong type of wormhole!

YOU CHOOSE Travel faster than a speeding bullet or become the world's first time traveller?

Would you rather discover extraterrestrial life ...

Are we alone?

You don't have to work for a secret government agency to hunt down alien life forms! All over the world, scientists are working together to look for signs of life elsewhere in the universe.

SETI is the Search for Extraterrestrial Intelligence. It focuses on signals from regions of space where there are Sun-like stars. It then analyses these signals to try to identify patterns that could indicate they were made by intelligent beings.

Hey! Over here!

No! Over here!

... or discover a new planet?

Become an armchair astronomer

Today, anyone with a computer can become an astronomer! Zooniverse is an online portal to a whole range of 'citizen science' projects, where the public can help scientists with research on both Earth- and space-focused projects.

Planet Hunters gets members of the public to study pictures from satellites and telescopes for signs of exoplanets. Galaxy Zoo asks people to look at telescope photos of distant galaxies and to classify them. Who knows – you might discover something amazing out there!

YOU CHOOSE Be a professional alien hunter or be the first to spot an alien world?

Would you rather the universe ended in a Big Crunch ...

Back to square one

Most scientists agree that the universe began with a Big Bang. At the start, the universe was a teeny, tiny dot. It grew at super speed – and it's still expanding today. Many scientists now believe that the universe will end in a kind of reverse Big Bang called the Big Crunch!

At some point, in the far-distant future, the universe will stop expanding. When it does, objects will start crashing into each other. The universe will get hotter and hotter until it shrinks back to a tiny (crunch) point.

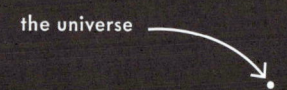

the universe

... or a Big Freeze?

Wrap up warm ready for the big chill

But not everyone agrees with the Big Crunch theory. Some scientists think that the universe will end with a Big Freeze – otherwise known as 'heat death'.

As the universe expands at a faster and faster rate, everything in it gets further and further apart. Eventually, stars won't be able to form, and the universe will cool down to a point where no heat energy exists at all. All movement will stop, and the universe will simply be a cold, dead space.

YOU CHOOSE Die in a sudden, dramatic collapse or endure a drawn-out, chilly end?

Would you rather climb Olympus Mons ...

A mountain more than twice as high as Mount Everest

Olympus Mons is a massive volcano on Mars. At around 25 kilometres high, it makes Everest, the tallest mountain on Earth, look like a little hill! It's the highest peak in the Solar System.

Mars is around half the size of Earth, so how did its volcanoes get so big? Scientists think that the volcanoes erupted for much longer, which helped them grow. Olympus Mons may have erupted for two million years! The lower strength of gravity on Mars may also have helped, allowing more magma to build higher up instead of pulling it down.

... or swim in Europa's ocean?

An ocean 15 times deeper than the deepest place on Earth

Beneath the icy surface of Jupiter's moon, Europa, lies an ocean that is unbelievably huge and unimaginably deep. There's more water on Europa than there is in all of Earth's oceans put together.

The deepest place on Earth is Challenger Deep in the Mariana Trench, which lies in the Pacific Ocean. It's a dark, mysterious place, more than 10 kilometres deep. But Europa's ocean beats that hands down. Scientists think it could be up to 150 kilometres deep in places!

YOU CHOOSE Hike to the summit of the Solar System or dive into its depths?

Would you rather take off in a rocket ...

Worse than the worst roller coaster you can imagine

The human body isn't really built for space travel. For example, when a rocket launches, it accelerates so fast that it applies huge force to the body. It pushes blood into your feet, away from the brain. You're more than likely to faint or throw up. Or both!

Astronauts are trained for months in machines called simulators. These recreate the same kind of conditions, noises and situations that the astronauts will experience during their journey, to help their bodies get used to it.

... or spend a few months on the International Space Station?

Become a sleepy weakling!

Living in space also takes a toll on the human body. Astronauts who spend a lot of time in microgravity, on the International Space Station, for example, have to take good care of themselves and do special exercises to keep their bodies working properly.

In space, with very little gravity to push against, muscles and bones get weaker. Fluids in the body also gather in the head, making your face look puffy and affecting your vision. Spending a long time in space can also be mentally challenging.

Wheeze!

YOU CHOOSE

Feel all your blood sinking to your feet or rushing to your head?

Would you rather spacewalk ...

A walk in the void

A spacewalk, or extravehicular activity (EVA), is when astronauts venture outside their space vehicle. Of course, they're not going out for a breath of fresh air! They only go outside to check and repair their spacecraft.

To survive a spacewalk, an astronaut wears a spacesuit. The suit's life-support system provides oxygen to breathe and to pressurise the suit. A spacesuit also contains water to drink. Astronauts are linked to the vehicle with a tether or move around using jetpacks.

... or moonwalk?

Fancy going for a lope?

With every step you take on Earth, you're acting against the force of gravity, which is pulling you towards the ground. That means you can move around without worrying about bouncing further than you intended!

The weaker gravity on the Moon makes it harder to go for a stroll, so astronauts use a different technique when they are there. They 'lope' or hop – a kind of bouncing stride – instead of walking. Pressurised spacesuits also help keep them closer to the ground.

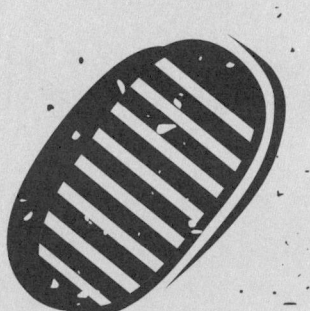

YOU CHOOSE Float like a butterfly or leap like a flea?

Would you rather spend winter on Neptune ...

Prepare to be frozen!

Neptune is a long, long way from the Sun – nearly 4.5 billion kilometres from it. That means it takes Neptune a very long time to make one full orbit of the Sun. One year on Neptune is 165 Earth years.

Of course, that means that each of the seasons on Neptune lasts a long time, too. Winter, spring, summer and autumn each last about 40 years. The average temperature on Neptune is a chilly −200° Celsius, so whichever season you visit in, pack a hat and scarf!

... or summer on Mercury?

Prepare to be fried!

The seasons on any planet are caused by the way it's tilted on its axis, so different parts of the planet receive different amounts of sunlight at different times of year. Unlike the other seven planets in the Solar System, Mercury has almost no tilt, so it doesn't have distinct seasons.

However, another unusual feature of Mercury is its highly elliptical orbit. The varying distances from the Sun that this creates does give Mercury a sort of summer and winter. At its closest point to the Sun, temperatures can reach 427° Celsius!

YOU CHOOSE A long, frozen winter or a short, fiery summer?

Would you rather try to eat in space ...

Could get messy!

Astronauts need to eat, but enjoying a meal in space is nothing like it is on Earth. To start with, simply sitting down is difficult in microgravity! The food has to be carefully prepared and packaged, so that it will last a long time and give astronauts the nutrients they need.

Some food, like nuts and biscuits, are packaged and ready to go. But other types of food are dehydrated – they have the liquid removed so they'll last longer – and astronauts have to add water to make them edible! They use straws to drink out of cartons, so liquids don't float around.

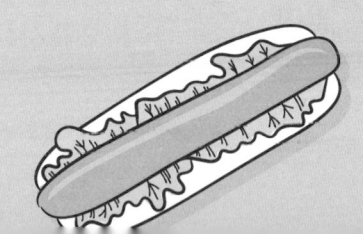

Zzzzz ...

... or sleep in space?

No chance of a good night's sleep!

There's no up or down in microgravity, so astronauts can sleep in any position they like! They tether themselves to something, so they don't float off in the night and bump into things.

One of the weirdest things about sleeping on the space station is that up there, night and day can be a bit confusing. The Sun rises and sets every 90 minutes on the space station, which can really mess up your sleep patterns!

YOU CHOOSE Faff around with floating food or tie yourself into bed?

Would you rather stare straight at a quasar ...

Cover your eyes

Quasar is short for 'quasi-stellar radio source'. A quasar is a region of light energy at the heart of a distant galaxy, surrounding a supermassive black hole.

You know how they say you should never stare directly at the Sun? Well, that rule would definitely apply to a quasar if you could get close to one! They're the brightest objects in the universe – trillions of times brighter than the Sun.

... or be sucked into a black hole?

A glimpse into the abyss

The most common black holes, stellar black holes, are up to about 20 times more massive than the Sun. But that's nothing compared to a supermassive black hole, whose mass can be millions of times bigger!

Black holes pull in anything that wanders too close, from entire stars to light itself. That's why we can't see black holes, because not even light can escape their gravity.

YOU CHOOSE Be blinded by the brightest light or tumble into eternal darkness?

Would you rather lose the Moon ...

Please don't lose the Moon!

THINK CRAB

CRABS ♥ MOON

More than just a lump of rock

The Moon might seem like it doesn't serve any purpose, but it's essential for life on Earth. Without the Moon, the tides would be much smaller. As a result, sea creatures such as crabs, mussels and starfish would die. That would have a knock-on effect on other ecosystems.

It also affects the seasons, because the pull of gravity between the Moon and Earth is what keeps our planet at a particular tilt. Without the Moon, Earth would tilt in different ways, causing extreme weather.

Hey, who turned the lights out?

... or have all the stars go out?

Star light, star bright, will the stars go out tonight?

The light we see from the most distant stars is ancient – those stars died long ago. But new stars are being born all the time, too. Light from the stars can be very useful. For example, people once used the stars' positions in the sky to help with navigation.

And don't forget that our own Sun is a star. If it went out, Earth would be a cold, dark, dead place!

YOU CHOOSE Put up with wild weather or permanent night?

Would you rather visit the Great Red Spot ...

No one could weather this storm!

The Great Red Spot is a huge storm on Jupiter. And you've never seen a hurricane like this! It's around 15,000 kilometres wide, which is nearly one and a half times as wide as Earth. It's been raging for about 200 years.

The storm gets its name because of how it looks in pictures – a big reddish blob moving in the planet's atmosphere. No one is totally sure why it looks red instead of white like hurricane clouds on Earth.

... or sunbathe in a sunspot?

Don't forget the sun cream!

Sunspots are patches on the surface of the Sun caused by magnetic activity. They're not stuck in one place, but can be seen moving across the Sun's surface, changing size and shape. Sunspots are actually very bright, but they're cooler than the rest of the surface and don't produce quite as much light as the area around them, so they look much darker.

People have observed sunspots for centuries. One early record is by a Chinese astronomer in CE 802, although he thought it was the planet Mercury passing across the Sun!

YOU CHOOSE Get blown about or suffer severe sunburn?

Would you rather discover the meaning of dark matter ...

There's a universe-sized hole in what we know

Think about everything we can see, know about and understand in the universe. That includes planets, stars, galaxies, black holes and every other space body, large and small. All of that makes up just 5 per cent of the universe.

The other 95 per cent is made up of what scientists call dark matter and dark energy. These consist of everything that has gravity, but which we can't see or understand. The amazing truth is that we really don't know what most of the universe actually is!

... or shed light on the dark side of the Moon?

Not such a dark secret after all

The dark side of the Moon sounds mysterious, but it's just another name for the far side of the Moon. People call it the 'dark side' because we never see it. In reality, it's no darker than the side we can see – the Sun shines on the far side, too!

The Moon spins on its axis at the same speed as it orbits Earth, so we always see the same side of it. We know what the far side looks like because spacecraft have flown past and taken pictures!

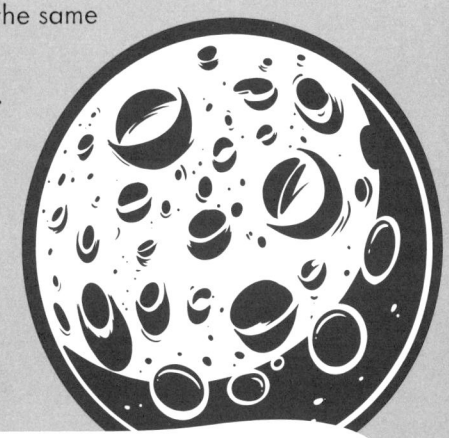

YOU CHOOSE Uncover the mysteries of the universe or see the Moon's secret side?

Would you rather be on a collision course with a galaxy ...

Brace yourself!

Galaxy collisions are more common than you might think. Our own galaxy, the Milky Way, is on a collision course with the Andromeda galaxy – although not for another 4–5 billion years!

In fact, there's so much space between objects that actual collisions are rare. Usually, the smaller galaxy gets 'eaten' by the bigger one, spitting out stars into space as it does so!

... or face an asteroid impact?

A ball of doom from space

A massive asteroid crash landing on Earth would kill millions of humans and animals immediately, of course. But living things that survived the impact would still face almost certain extinction.

An asteroid impact would send up clouds of gas and dust into the atmosphere, which would block out the Sun completely. With no Sun, no plants could grow. Without plants, animals cannot survive.

YOU CHOOSE Get gobbled up by a galaxy or slowly starve on Earth?

Hmm, that's a big one ...

Would you rather get fried by a flare ...

A hot life fuelled by a red dwarf

Red dwarf stars are the most common stars in the universe, and the ones that live longest. Red dwarves are cool and dim – too dim to be seen from Earth with the naked eye. They're less than half the mass of our Sun, which is classified as a yellow dwarf.

Unfortunately, it wouldn't be great to have a red dwarf at the heart of your solar system. This is mainly because they have a lot of solar flares, which would make nearby planets too toasty to live on!

... or never evolve?

Fancy a blue giant for a sun?

Blue giants are among the biggest, hottest stars in the universe. They give off a huge amount of energy, too: around 10,000 times more than our Sun.

Unfortunately, because of their giant mass they use up their fuel very quickly. So, supergiant stars don't live very long compared to other stars – only 10–50 million years. That's not long enough for life to evolve very far, and certainly not to the point we've reached on Earth!

YOU CHOOSE — A hot life or a short life?

Would you rather take a space holiday in the mountains ...

Climb the mountains of Io

Io is one of Jupiter's moons, and it's absolutely covered in mountains and active volcanoes. In fact, Io is the most volcanically active body in the Solar System, sometimes shooting scalding gas more than 300 kilometres into space!

There are also around 135 mountains on Io. The tallest is South Boösaule Mons, which, at 17,500 metres, is more than twice the height of Mount Everest. Unlike on Earth, most of Io's mountains don't form in ranges, but sprout up individually all over its surface.

... or go on a lakeside retreat?

Sail on Titan's lakes

Saturn's moon Titan is covered in lakes. But instead of being filled with water, they're made up of methane and ethane. On Earth these are gases, but in the chilly temperatures of Titan, they form as liquids.

The lakes seem to be created by rain and by the liquids rising from below ground. But beware! If you tried to sail in them, your boat would sink like a stone, because it would be so much heavier than the liquid methane and ethane.

YOU CHOOSE Climb for your life or drown in freezing liquid?

Would you rather get caught in Venus's rain ...

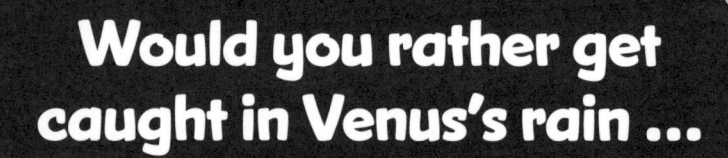

Err, that umbrella may not help!

Severe weather warning!

The planet Venus is home to some very wild weather. Not only is it the hottest planet in the Solar System, it also experiences strong winds and lightning storms.

But the worst of it is the rain. High in Venus's atmosphere linger clouds of sulphuric acid, so it rains acid drops! On the bright side, it's so hot on Venus that the acid rain would evaporate before it reached the surface.

... or Neptune's winds?

Whoa! This is a bit TOO exciting!

A great planet for kite-flying!

Neptune claims the title of windiest planet. There, the methane winds whip faster than the speed of sound. They move so fast partly because Neptune is such a flat planet – there's nothing to slow the gusts down.

Neptune also has storms similar to Jupiter's Great Red Spot. The Great Dark Spot spins around, disappearing and reappearing. In 2018, a smaller companion storm was spotted, which astronomers called Dark Spot Jr!

YOU CHOOSE Have your skin sizzled by acid rain or get blown about by a stinky, supersonic wind?

Would you rather spin around a spiral galaxy ...

Let's go for a whirl!

Galaxies are named for their shapes: spiral, elliptical and irregular. Spiral galaxies contain lots of young stars in 'arms' moving outwards in a spiral. They also have a flat disc of stars in the middle. A the heart of a spiral galaxy lies a supermassive black hole.

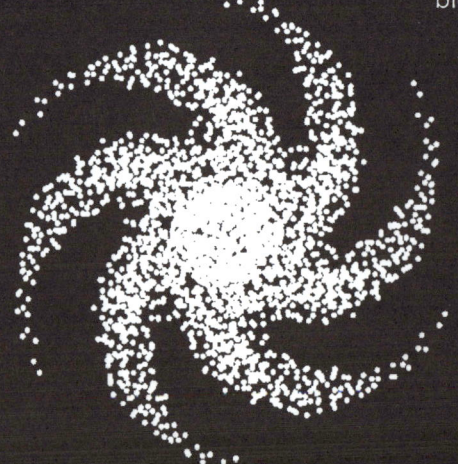

Our Solar System is positioned in the arm of a spiral galaxy called the Milky Way, about 26,000 light years from the centre. Our galaxy spins at a speedy 200 kilometres per second!

... or orbit an elliptical galaxy?

A diverse group of galaxies

Elliptical galaxies are round or oval, and they don't have 'arms' like spiral galaxies. They range in size from dwarf galaxies, only one-tenth of the size of the Milky Way, to huge galaxies more than a million light years across. And they're filled with mysterious dark matter!

Stars in elliptical galaxies seem to be more evenly spaced out than in spiral galaxies. They also tend to be older and have lower masses. One feature that they do share with spiral galaxies is the supermassive black hole in the middle.

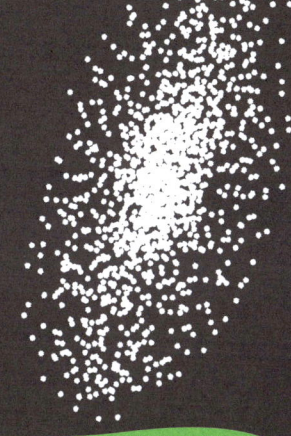

YOU CHOOSE See what happens to young stars on a spiral arm or old stars in an ancient galaxy?

Would you rather be a cosmologist ...

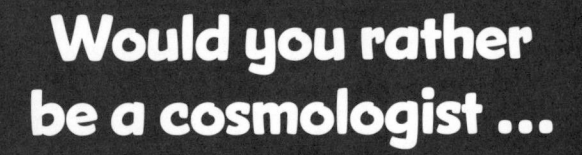

They do bang on about their theories!

There are lots of different jobs you can do if you're seriously into space – astronaut, astronomer, aerospace engineer, researcher ... But take note, you'll have to pay attention in science lessons!

A cosmologist is a scientist who studies how the universe began and how it has developed, and what might happen in the future. Cosmologists study the big picture, trying to understand the whole universe. One of the biggest theories they work with is the Big Bang.

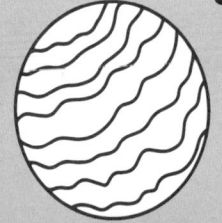

... or an astrophysicist?

They've got an answer for everything!

Astrophysicists are super-smart scientists who explain how and why the universe is the way it is. Astrophysicists and astronomers rely on each other's work for their own studies.

Ah, yes, I thought so ...

Astronomers look at the position and movement of objects in space, from planets and stars to nebulae and black holes. Astrophysicists are experts in the laws of physics, so they use these to explain why these objects move and behave the way they do.

YOU CHOOSE Delve into the secrets of the past and future, or explain the evidence of your own eyes?

Would you rather go gold mining on an asteroid ...

Striking gold in space

There's loads of gold in the universe. A lot of it can be found on asteroids, where precious metals and minerals aren't buried as deep as they are on Earth. Still, it wouldn't be easy to go mining on an asteroid that's spinning and wobbling through space!

One particular asteroid, 16 Psyche, has so much gold it's got scientists excited. They think this might be part of the core planetesimal – the building block of a planet. This could tell us what Earth's core looks like. NASA is planning to send a probe to the asteroid to find out more ...

... or diamond mining on another planet?

A precious planet

The planet 55 Cancri e is in our own galaxy, the Milky Way. It's also a 'super-Earth' – a planet larger than Earth, but smaller than Neptune.

When scientists first found 55 Cancri e, they were very excited by the amount of diamond and the mineral graphite it contained. Although they now believe there's less diamond than originally thought, the idea of a 'diamond planet' caught people's imaginations. And you wouldn't even have to do too much digging, as temperatures on 55 Cancri e are hot enough to melt rock!

YOU CHOOSE Be a gold digger on a fast-moving rock or sparkle in the superheat of a super-Earth?

Would you rather be caught in a solar flare ...

Watch out for a flare-up!

Solar flares are huge explosions on the surface of the Sun. They happen when energy from magnetic fields is suddenly released, so they're basically big bursts of radiation. They contain about as much energy as one billion nuclear bombs!

The Sun is a very long way from Earth, but don't think you're safe from a solar flare! Sometimes a coronal mass ejection (CME) occurs. This can send millions of tonnes of matter out into space – which can even reach Earth.

... or in the solar wind?

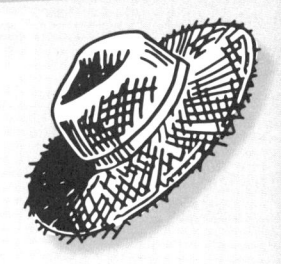

Hold on to your hat!

Solar winds are streams of particles that are thrown out from the Sun's outer atmosphere, called the corona. They travel so fast, around 1.6 million kilometres per hour, that they can bend Earth's magnetic field!

Solar winds are also responsible for the aurora – the amazing dancing lights in the sky. These lights, seen most clearly near the North and South Poles, are caused when charged particles in the solar wind interact with Earth's magnetic field.

YOU CHOOSE Experience a fiery eruption on the Sun or dancing lights on Earth?

Would you rather be stuck in the pitch-black ...

Who's afraid of the dark?

Exoplanet TrES-2 b is the darkest planet ever discovered. This gas giant, about the same size as Jupiter, only reflects about 1 per cent of the light that hits it from the star it orbits. If a spacecraft entered the planet's atmosphere, it would literally be flying blind.

I can't see where we're going!

TrES-2 b is very hot – its atmosphere is around 980° Celsius. Because of its heat, the planet may emit a faint, eerie red glow, like embers in a lump of coal.

... or on a planet on a path to destruction?

A frying egg

WASP-12 b is an exoplanet classed as a 'hot Jupiter'. It's about twice the size of that planet and definitely earns the title 'hot', with temperatures reaching an unbearable 2,210° Celsius.

But the most unusual thing about WASP-12 b is that it's being torn apart by the gravitational pull of the star it's orbiting. The huge star is stretching the planet into an egg shape, as well as pulling chunks of it into its own mass!

I can't take this pressure – I'm going to crack!

YOU CHOOSE: Be stuck in eternal night or watch as a star sucks you towards your doom?

Would you rather see the dawn of the universe ...

What lies beyond?

Since the moment of the Big Bang, the universe has been getting bigger. It's been expanding in all directions for 13.8 billion years. What's really mind-boggling, though, is that the universe is now – and always has been – infinite, so there's no edge for us to see.

However, we can see the universe as it was in the past. Telescopes like Hubble and the James Webb Space Telescope are sort of time machines. By taking images of the distant universe, they're showing us what was going on billions of years ago.

... or see the Great Barrier Reef from space?

A different view

From a prime position in space, you can see lots of things on Earth, from swirling hurricane clouds to the Himalayan Mountains to the Pyramids of Giza in Egypt.

The largest living thing that you can spot from space is the Great Barrier Reef, which runs for more than 2,000 kilometres off the east coast of Australia. The colour of the reef stands out from the darker blue of the surrounding sea.

YOU CHOOSE Peer into the past or get a new perspective on your home planet?

Would you rather have a protostar as a night light ...

This little one might keep you up at night

A protostar is a baby star, one at the start of its life cycle. At this stage, it's a cold cloud of hydrogen gas. Childhood lasts a long time for stars – about 500,000 years. During this time, they gather mass until they become fully formed stars.

But being young and cool doesn't mean being dim. Some protostars are really bright, and actually lose some of their luminosity when they become adult stars on what scientists call the 'main sequence'.

... or a planetesimal as a pet?

How Earth began ...

Planetesimals are small, solid space bodies made of dust and gas. They form around young stars, as pieces of dust collide and clump together. All the planets in the Solar System may have started life as planetesimals.

The name might make you think these are small, cute space bodies. But they're not that small. In fact, some of them grow to be a few hundred kilometres wide.

YOU CHOOSE — Take care of a baby star or a baby planet?

Would you rather swim in the Sea of Tranquility ...

Probably as peaceful as it sounds!

You'd struggle to swim in the Sea of Tranquility, because it isn't actually a sea. The 'seas' on the Moon were called this by early astronomers who couldn't see them in detail and thought they were water. In fact, they're large plains made of a dark rock called basalt, which were formed by ancient asteroid impacts.

When NASA was planning the Moon landings back in the 1960s, it chose the Sea of Tranquility as the landing site because it was a flat, smooth area. It was also the right temperature for the astronauts to work in, and it looked like it had some interesting dust and rocks to bring back to Earth!

... or splash around in Enceladus's ocean?

You'll want to wear a wetsuit!

Saturn's moon Enceladus is nicknamed the 'ocean moon', because beneath its crust is an entire saltwater ocean! Vents in the moon's crust shoot out jets of freezing liquid particles hundreds of kilometres into space.

Although Enceladus is only 500 kilometres across, it's really bright. In fact, it's the most reflective body in the Solar System. For a long time, scientists couldn't figure out why. Now they know it's because of its smooth, icy, white surface.

YOU CHOOSE Take a dusty dip on our own Moon or a cold shower on Saturn's moon?

Would you rather be pulled into a magnetic field ...

Can you feel the attraction?

A magnetar is a really powerful neutron star. *Super* powerful. A magnetar's magnetic field is a trillion times stronger than Earth's. If you got too close – say within 1,000 kilometres of it – you'd suffer a gruesome death. All your atoms would stretch, and soon your body would just ... disappear.

Magnetars are still a bit of a mystery to space scientists. No one known where their huge power comes from – or why they release so much energy in flares and huge bursts of radiation.

... or exposed to cosmic radiation?

Dangerous rays from space

Cosmic radiation is made up of high-energy particles that shoot down to Earth at the speed of light from beyond our Solar System. They're mostly particles called protons. If they all made it right down to Earth, the human race would be in trouble.

Fortunately, we're protected from cosmic radiation as long as we keep our feet firmly on Earth. An area of space around our planet, called the magnetosphere, deflects most of the dangerous cosmic rays. A few particles get through, but not enough to cause any harm.

YOU CHOOSE Be vaporised by magnetism or harmed by radiation?

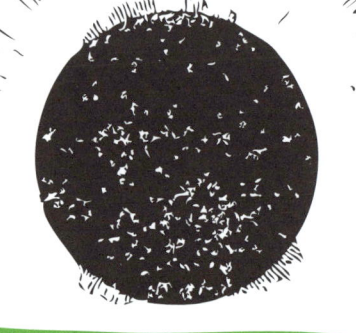

Would you rather live with a permanent solar eclipse ...

Get ready for a blackout

A solar eclipse happens when the Moon moves between Earth and the Sun. It blocks out the Sun's light, cloaking our planet in shadow. There are two main types of solar eclipse: partial and total.

A partial eclipse is when part of the Sun can still be seen over the edge of the Moon. A total eclipse happens when the Sun and Moon perfectly align. The Sun is about 400 times bigger than the Moon, but the Moon is 400 times closer to Earth, so they look about the same size.

... or a permanent lunar eclipse?

It casts a long shadow

A lunar eclipse takes place when the Moon is positioned on the exact opposite side of Earth to the Sun. Lunar eclipses only happen when the Moon is full.

During a lunar eclipse, Earth's shadow (called the umbra) falls on the Moon. Some sunlight still reaches the surface of the Moon through the atmosphere, but usually only the colours with longer wavelengths, such as orange and red. This often turns the Moon an eerie colour, like it's covered in blood!

YOU CHOOSE Life in the gloom or with a gory Moon?

Would you rather see a planet with two suns ...

Grab your shades – it'll be twice as bright!

Double suns might seem like the stuff of science fiction, but there are millions of them. These binary star systems happen when two stars close together are joined by the mutual pull of their gravity. Astronomers think that maybe half of the stars in the Milky Way are in binary systems!

Some binary star systems even have their own planets. So far astronomers know of about 100 of these planetary systems. They're nicknamed 'Tatooine' planets after Luke Skywalker's home planet in the *Star Wars* films!

... or a sun with two planets?

A solar system like our own?

Lots of stars probably have planets orbiting them, like the set-up in our own Solar System. They might even be able to support life! The problem is that it's hard to see the planets because they don't give off any light of their own.

Until recently, we only knew that multiple-planet systems existed because they make the star they're moving around wobble. But in 2020, astronomers snapped the first photographs of a sunlike star orbited by two planets, called TYC 8998-760-1 b and c.

YOU CHOOSE Live like a Skywalker or see a place where life might one day develop?

Would you rather have a birthday party on Venus ...

Celebrate every day!

On Venus, a day is longer than a year. Hard to get your head around? Well, a day is the time it takes for a planet to make one full spin on its axis (24 hours on Earth). A year is the time it takes for the planet to travel round the Sun. On Earth, that's 365.25 days.

Time passes differently on Venus. A year is only 225 Earth days there, but it takes Venus 243 days to spin once on its axis. So in a weird way, it would be your birthday every day!

Happy Birthday!

Happy Birthday again!

Err, and again!

... or a New Year's Eve party on Mercury?

Doesn't time fly?

Mercury is the closest planet to the Sun, which means it has the shortest year. On Mercury, a year lasts just 88 Earth days. So, New Year's Eve would come around at the equivalent of every three months on Earth.

Of course, with the years passing by so quickly on both planets, you'd age faster – 1.6 times as fast on Venus and four times as fast on Mercury!

YOU CHOOSE One party a day or one party a season?

GLOSSARY

asteroid a small, rocky space body that orbits the Sun, sometimes called a minor planet or planetoid

atmosphere the layer of gases that surround a planet

axis an imaginary line through the middle of something like a planet, around which its spins

basalt a type of rock formed when lava from volcanoes cools and hardens

chemical element a substance that is made up of just one type of atom; elements cannot be broken down into simpler substances

circumference the distance all the way round the outside of something, such as a planet

comet a lump of ice, dust and rock that orbits the Sun

dwarf planet a small, planet-like body in space that has enough gravity to have been pulled into a ball shape, but not enough to have cleared the neighbourhood of its orbit of other space bodies

ecosystem all the living and non-living things that exist in a particular area or environment

exoplanet a planet that orbits a star outside our own Solar System

greenhouse gas a gas in the atmosphere, such as carbon dioxide or methane, that traps heat and causes a planet to warm up

horizon the line where the sky and Earth seem to meet when you look into the distance

hypothetical describing something based on an idea that has not yet been proven by facts

luminosity a measure of how bright a star is

magnetar a neutron star with a very strong magnetic field

meteor small pieces of matter from space that enter Earth's atmosphere and look like streaks of light

meteorite a rock from space that has survived the journey through our atmosphere to land on Earth

meteoroid a small object made of rock or metals that orbits the Sun

microgravity very weak gravity, such as that on a space station

minerals solid substances that occur naturally on Earth and on other planets

neutron star a small, dense space body formed from the collapse of a giant star

nucleus the main part of a comet, made of ice and gas along with some dust and rock particles

nutrients substances that humans and other living things need in order to grow and be healthy

particles tiny pieces of matter

planetesimal a small space body made of gas and dust

GLOSSARY

probe a spacecraft that has no human pilot

proton a tiny particle that exists in the nucleus of an atom

protostar a star in the early stages of its life cycle

radiation energy that moves from place to place; heat and light are both forms of radiation

rogue planet a planet that does not orbit a star, but instead floats freely in space

simulators machines that recreate specific conditions, such as microgravity or high pressure, to train astronauts for space missions

tectonic plates the broken pieces of Earth's crust that are constantly moving around

tether a long cable that keeps an astronaut attached to a spacecraft while they are working outside it

wavelength the distance between the peaks of two waves, usually applied to electromagnetic waves

Further information

Books

The Truth About Space (Fact or Fake?)
by Sonya Newland (Wayland, 2022)

A Guide to Space by Kevin Pettman (Wayland, 2019)

Space (Infomojis)
by Jon Richards and Ed Simkins (Wayland, 2018)

Space (Adventures in STEAM)
by Richard Spilsbury (Capstone Press, 2018)

Websites

www.esa.int/kids/en/home
Explore space further with the European Space Agency's website.

spaceplace.nasa.gov/
Find out more about every space topic imaginable at NASA's Space Place.

spotthestation.nasa.gov/
Use this website to help you spot the International Space Station as it orbits overhead.

voyager.jpl.nasa.gov/mission/status/
Follow the Voyager spacecraft on their journey through interstellar space, with real-time tracking from NASA.

INDEX

Andromeda 60
Asteroid Belt 6, 7
asteroids 5, 6, 21, 34, 61, 72, 82
astronauts 27, 31, 44, 45, 46, 50, 51, 70
astronomers 39, 57, 70, 71, 82, 88, 89
astrophysics 71
atmosphere 4, 16, 18, 21, 24, 29, 32, 56, 61, 66, 87

Big Bang 40, 70, 78
Big Crunch 40, 41
Big Freeze 41
black holes 28, 37, 52, 53, 58, 68, 69, 71

Ceres 6, 13
comets 7, 11, 20, 21, 34

dark matter 58, 69
diamond 73
dwarf planets 6, 7, 13

Earth 4, 10, 11, 14, 15, 16, 18, 21, 24, 25, 26, 29, 30, 32, 39, 42, 47, 54, 55, 56, 59, 61, 62, 63, 64, 65, 72, 73, 74, 75, 79, 84, 85, 86, 87, 90, 91
eclipses 86, 87
Enceladus 83
Eris 13
Europa 35, 43
event horizon 28
exoplanets 32, 33, 76, 77

galaxies 36, 39, 52, 58, 60, 61, 68, 69, 73
Galileo 35
gold 72, 73

gravity 8, 9, 10, 11, 13, 15, 24, 25, 28, 34, 42, 45, 47, 50, 51, 53, 54, 58, 77, 88
Great Dark Spot 67
Great Red Spot 56, 67

helium 8, 19
hydrogen 8, 15, 19, 80

Io 35, 64

Jupiter 6, 11, 12, 19, 23, 32, 35, 43, 56, 64, 77

Kuiper Belt 7

life 27, 38, 54, 61, 63, 89
light 28, 29, 36, 53, 55
litter 30

magnetars 84
magnetic field 22, 74, 75, 84
Mars 6, 25, 27, 42
Mercury 4, 18, 49, 57
meteorites 21
meteoroids 16, 21
meteors 16
methane 15, 65, 67
Milky Way, the 60, 68, 69, 73, 88
Moon, the 6, 10, 17, 18, 24, 47, 54, 59, 82, 83, 86, 87
moons 17, 34, 35, 43, 64, 65, 83

nebulae 8, 71
Neptune 5, 7, 23, 48, 67, 73

oceans 19, 43, 83

planetesimals 72, 81
Pluto 7, 13
protostars 80

quasars 52

rain 32, 33, 65, 66, 67
rings 23, 34
rogue planets 12

Saturn 23, 34, 83
seasons 17, 48, 49, 54
solar flares 62, 74
Solar System, the 4, 7, 12, 20, 21, 24, 42, 43, 49, 64, 66, 68, 81, 83, 85, 89
space stations 31, 45, 51
spacecraft 24, 26, 44, 46, 59, 76
spacesuits 24, 46, 47
stars 8, 9, 12, 16, 36, 38, 55, 58, 62, 63, 71, 77, 80, 88, 89
Sun, the 4, 5, 10, 13, 18, 19, 20, 48, 51, 52, 53, 55, 57, 59, 61, 62, 74, 75, 86, 87, 90, 91
sunspots 57
supernovae 9

telescopes 39, 78
terminator, the 29
Titan 65

Uranus 5, 23, 78

Venus 4, 22, 23, 66, 90, 91
volcanoes 42, 64

winds 33, 66, 67, 75
wormholes 37

96